MW01656839

JUST FO

21-Day Devotional

Dominique Duncan

Copyright © 2019 Dominique Duncan

All rights reserved. No part of this book may be used or reproduced by any means, graphic, electronic, or mechanical, including photocopying, recording, taping or by any information storage retrieval system without the written permission of the author except in the case of brief quotations embodied in critical articles and reviews.

Because of the dynamic nature of the Internet, any web addresses or links contained in this book may have changed since publication and may no longer be valid. The views expressed in this work are solely those of the author and do not necessarily reflect the views of the publisher, and the publisher hereby disclaims any responsibility for them.

All Scripture quotations are taken from the New King James Version ®. Copyright © 1982 by Thomas Nelson. Used by permission. All rights reserved.

ISBN: 978-1-0868-0616-8

Thank you, Jesus!

To Jelani & JP, I do this for you!

Love, Mommy

Just for Today...

Dear Reader,

Ever felt like you were not enough? I have. I have been struggling between two decisions. Whether to stay where I was being loved deprived or take a step out on faith and finally I choose me. I had finally realized that change would only happen if I did the changing. So many years I thought that if such and such loved me, then I would be better. I found myself enjoying those who didn't care and hurting those who did care. I loved from the outside in, instead of from the inside out. My decisions based on if I did this right Daddy would love me for me, or if I fixed this Momma would be proud. I was allowing people's perception of me to determine who I was. It became so bad that I began to "love" people for their potential instead of who they were. I was pushing off what I thought love was because of what I experienced. I was in a love drought. I had no desire in me to give, so instead, I was giving out dust as a symbol of my love for those who didn't even like me. I loved those who didn't love me because I didn't love me.

I was choosing people who didn't even have me on their list as a choice. I couldn't understand why I was not called for group outings, brunch dates, or why I wasn't being picked to be on the team. That's because I was wasting my love for undeserving people. I was too focused on being accepted by the wrong people that I missed the opportunity to be loved by the right people.

Love is a form of communication. Which means it's a two-way street. People say talking to someone who cares less about you is like talking to a brick wall. Well, what do you think about loving someone who doesn't love you? I had to finally pull myself together with the help of Jesus and find out why I was in need of being accepted and not loved. I had finally had enough. I was an empty jar trying to pour out what I didn't have in me into someone else. I didn't get ticked off, but finally, I was ticked on. I had to CHOOSE ME finally!

I was so busy trying to get everyone else to choose something that I wasn't even trying to choose. Moreover, that was ME. First, how could I persuade someone to want something that I didn't believe? Second, once I finally chose me, having to convince you to choose me was out of the question. Third, if you rejected me, that was your loss, not mine. Lastly, I realized that I was never to empty myself for someone else. However, I was to give them the overflow of what I already had inside of me.

My husband and children were suffering from the lack of love I had for myself. I had had enough. So I decided to *Choose Me*, finally. After looking in the mirror every morning before or after I washed my face and telling the beautiful chick in the mirror that I loved her, life became better. I was filling the void with the love of God and self. I filled it with verses like, "I will praise You, for I am fearfully and wonderfully made; Marvelous are your works, and that my soul knows very well," (Psalm 139:14) "I have said, Ye are gods; and all of you are children of the Most High" (Psalm 82:6) and "But now, says the Lord—the one who created you, Jacob, the one who formed you, Israel: Don't fear, for I have redeemed you; I have called you by name; you are mine." (Isaiah 43:1)

Acceptance became less of a motive, and love became more of a lifestyle. I chose myself with all my flaws. Also, I continue to choose me each day I wake up. So choose you even if no man does. Choose you and continue to Choose You.

I challenge you to look in the mirror for 21 days and tell yourself you love you. In those same 21 days, study what God says about you. Take sticky notes and place them in the mirror so that you can see what He says about you every morning. Lastly, make a list of 21 things you love. Each day must be something new. As you read this, Just for Today Devotion, my prayer is that you work it. This devotional will only work if you work it and allow God's spirit to intervene in the rest. Twenty-one days will be hard, but I believe the spirit of consistency will prevail.

I love you!

Be Blessed

Dominique Duncan

Prayer: Thank you, Lord! Thank you for just being you. Thank you for loving us even when we didn't know how to love. Thank you for showing us what and who love is. Your word, God, says, "But seek first his kingdom and his righteousness, and all these things will be given to you as well." Thank you for the grace and mercy while we were in a state of ignorance and rebellion. Jesus, I bind the spirit of low self-esteem and the sense of self-

rejection of every reader and those connected to them. I plead the blood against every demonic influence that tells them lies. Lord, help us to have DIVINE CONNECTIONS. Allow those to complement what you have already made and said through your word. Thank you for your Love, Compassion, and Healing power in our broken season. I bless you and honor you, My Savior, My Deliverer, My Healer, My King. Thank you for every reader. I pray, Lord, that you enrich every reader with your spirit and with the words that you have guided my hands to write. Thank you, Jesus! We love You! In Jesus' name, I pray, Amen!

Day 1

"Therefore do not worry about tomorrow, for tomorrow will worry about its own things. Sufficient for the day is its own trouble" Matthew 6:34

Hakuna Matata! It means No Worries, according to Disney's Lion King. How many of us wish we had no worries? Well, guess what you do. Matthew 6:25-34 is a whole section where Jesus gives us the command of "Do Not Worry." I know it's better said than done; especially if you picked up this book.

Nevertheless, it was a command from Jesus. I know, of all the things I could start this devotional off with I chose the command of Do Not Worry. When worry is what may have brought you here. It was the frustration you had with your addicted spouse. It was the hurt from the family drama you deal with. Or maybe it was just the title that brought you here. So, what now? You're hurt, and you have nothing to do but keep replaying in your mind how you should handle the circumstance. Do me a favor and RELEASE IT! That's right, release it to God. Jesus says in Matthew 6:34 that tomorrow has its own problem, so why stress and bring about health issues if not more? The command "Do Not Worry" wasn't optional. However, He did give you an option to be obedient or not. You see, you were worried about what to do next, but God said to release it to me so that I can do what I want to do for you.

I realized that the best answer to live with is when Jesus says yes. Living in the yes requires an attitude of Hakuna Matata! Can you handle that? Can you cast your cares on the Lord? Why not? He already cares for you and has his hands out ready to help you release those worries unto him. Be free and watch how easy it will be going God's way without a concern.

Just for today, I will try my best to live unafraid. I will release my worries and request patience, joy, and endurance. I will enjoy what is beautiful on this day.

Prayer: Thank You, Jesus! Today I release my worries to you. Your Word says to cast our cares unto you because you care. As we release our fears, we request patience and joy to endure this race you have placed us in. Thank you in advance!

Have your way in our lives as we surrender to you.

I pray this in Jesus' name. Amen!

Day 2

"The Lord will fight for you, and you shall hold your peace." Exodus 14:14

Growing up as an only child, things that were normal for me changed when I met my father and my three siblings. I'm used to fighting alone and never really having someone to help me. I learned that I was going to fight hard and win, or I was going to take a loss like a champ. I had cousins, but I only saw them on weekends or whenever my mother would travel to East Baltimore to see them. One day when I was 12 visiting my father, my older sister had a friend who kept picking on my younger sister. My older sister told my younger sister to stand still and that she would handle the issue. After a while, I realized that my older sister was fighting the person who kept picking up my younger sister at the playground. I was so amazed that my little sister didn't even have to fight because she had someone willing to fight for her.

Imagine you being that little sister and how the enemy has been messing with you. He has been messing with your health, finances, family, and or your business that you've worked so hard to build. Here in Exodus, Moses tells the people of Israel to hold still because God was going to fight their battles. As it was for them in the Old Testament, I am here to tell you that promise is still applicable within our everyday lives. I know it has been rough for a few days, months, or even years. Just stand still, because God shall fight for you. The best part of that scripture is that God says you shall be able to hold your peace. Many times, under challenging circumstances, our peace is usually the first thing to go. God tells us, if you let me fight this I promise your peace will not be taken from you!

Just for today, I release my control and standstill. I stand on the promise that God shall fight my battles for me and that my peace will remain stable.

Prayer: Father God, thank you for the peace you've given me during this trial. Thank you for fighting my battles. Lord, I release my control, and I hand this fight to you. For it is in your word that you shall fight for me. I trust you fully. Thank you in advance for victory because I know that it is mine. I pray this in Jesus' Name, Amen!

Day 3

"Be Anxious for nothing, but in everything by prayer and supplication, with thanksgiving, let your request be made known to God; and the peace of God, which surpasses all understanding, will guard your hearts and minds through Christ Jesus"

Philippians 4:6-7

Here I am in the process of buying a house, and things have been going good so far. I have my closing date, I received a grant, and here's where things began to get weird. So this grant I received, although it would cover my closing costs and a portion of my down payment, there is still more for me to pay. I am nervous because at this very moment I have no clue where the extra funds will come from but as I sit here in my stress to figure it out; this scripture came to mind. Many people write devotionals and books after they go through. God stopped me and said write this from your experience today. I do not know where the money will come from, I do not see how it will come, and I do not know when but what I do know is" WHO!

I know for many of you it's the not knowing that makes us anxious, but the scripture says don't even worry about that. Yet, it's the unanswered questions that make us worry. Not only does Paul tell us not to be anxious, but he also gives us directions on what to do with nothing. He tells us to take that "*nothing*" and turn it into prayer and praise. He explains to give God those unanswered questions. The questions how, when, and what are to be turned into THANK YOU! When roadblocks come up in your situations with family, health, finances, or even like me, promotion; begin to thank him for what he has already done AND for what you believe him for. The scripture doesn't just end with telling us to thank him; it says to let our request be made known.

I promise if you start thanking him for the situation you will feel better. This is not just a saying, but scripture tells us that once we start thanking Him for what we have and what we believe him for then the peace of God will come and guard our hearts and minds. We may not know what will happen or when until it happens but what we can do is thank Him while we wait. Remember, wait is a verb. W.A.I.T or What Am I Thinking/Talking? Use this time to think and talk thanksgiving! Remember he may not come when you want Him, but He is an on-time God!

Just for today, I will think and talk thanksgiving!

Prayer: Father, Thank you! Thank you for everything. We thank you for what we have and what you plan to give! We thank you for who you are to us now and who you shall be for us forever! We thank you for everything you did, what you are doing, and what you plan to do! Thank you, Jesus! Amen!

Day 4

"Therefore I say to you, whatever things you ask when you pray, believe that you receive them, and you will have them." Mark 11:24

I struggled with asking for things from people. I just always felt me asking would make them feel bothered or cause them to walk away. Yes, that meant even from family, romantic relationships and close friendships. After a while, I became frustrated with the feeling that my feelings were not being heard. It wasn't anyone else's fault but my own because I was too afraid to ask for what I needed. One day I asked a friend to be a little gentle with speaking to me in specific ways. This person did not like what was said, so they stopped dealing with me. Even though it was for the best, I was still hurt. Aren't you glad God doesn't shun us when we ask for specific things? The good thing is that when we ask for anything; God promises that we will have it. Of course, I am sure this is within boundaries. God is not a genie where we rub his lamp, and he grants our three wishes. He is more significant than that.

I know when you read this, you were thinking of that big house you saw, or that nice car, or even that sexy looking spouse you saw. Now I am not saying that this can't happen, but here in this text, Jesus is speaking of the hard things. Let's talk about some things that we struggle with. How about that disease that just won't go away? That loved one who struggles with addiction? Battling infertility? When you just can't get out of the red in your financial situation? Or the generational curse you can't seem to shake? God is saying have faith and speak to that mountain, without doubt, and watch it be removed. The directions are clear, although I know some things are easier said than done. The instructions to speak, don't doubt, but believe are hard to follow when you've been stuck in your struggle for days, months, or even years.

Nevertheless, these directions are necessary so that verse 24 can happen. The only way for us to see what we speak is to pray and believe. There is no room for doubt. The ball is in your court. You're either going to trust Him or not. So, whose report will you believe?

Just for today, I will believe in what I prayed for entirely — no doubting one bit.

Prayer: God, thank you! Thank you for the hard thing that shall be taken care of by you. Today I pray for_______(struggle), and I give it to you. I stand on your word that whatever I pray for and believe it shall come to pass in your name. I thank you in advance for the manifestation in Jesus' name. I plead the blood against anything that will try to deny me. I pray this in Jesus' name. Amen!

Day 5

"When the time is right, I, the Lord, will come quickly. I will make these things happen." Isaiah 60:22b

"NO!" How many of us heard this word from others when we knew the time had to be right? I know I have, many times. I've listened to this word so much that I just started to believe that people were going to say no before I even asked. It got so bad that I stopped asking because I was afraid of the word, "NO." I began to feel like I was failing at life because all I knew were the words No, Nope, Nah, Not yet, or Never. N-words begin to plague my life. But God! I know many of you can stop right there and give God praise. I learned that even though man said “No,” didn't mean it was over. I think we forget the verse Isaiah 60:22 when man says the No. No one can stop what The Lord allows to happen or what he plans to do in our lives. What we must do is trust God's timing.

Sometimes the timing may not be right. This scripture makes us the promise that when the time is right and righteous that Jesus shall come quickly. I remember when I first got preapproved for a house. For three years straight, I was getting the N-words, No, Nope and Not Yet. I became so discouraged that I thought homeownership just wasn't in my destiny. When it was my time and my turn things begin to happen so quickly. I was pre-approved on a Monday, on Wednesday I went looking for a house, Thursday I put a contract on the house and by that night I was under contract. The owners only took 15 minutes to accept it. I was expecting more like 2-3 days. I knew that it was my time and my turn by what God had allowed to happen. The right timing will produce a quickness of manifestation. It will happen so quickly that you will forget that it really took years on your calendar. God's timing is ALWAYS RIGHT! When it's your time and your turn with God, he will make things happen faster than you know it. It will have you feeling like blessings are just flooding in your lap. Trust God's timing!

Just for today, I will save myself from hurry, and indecision. I will allow God's plan for my life to manifest through my surrendering.

Prayer: Father, I surrender it all to you! Have your way in my life. Let my timing submit to you

and your schedule. For I know, your calendar is right. I love you, and I trust you. In Jesus' name, Amen!

Day 6

"For let, not that man suppose that he will receive anything from the Lord; he is a double-minded man, unstable in all his ways." James 1:7-8

For the past few years, I was so unstable in everything I pursued. I was so confused about what to do with my life and who to listen to. Recently, having a conversation with my mentor, I explained to her that I took her advice and wise counsel for granted. I did, and I was deeply apologetic about it. I was so immature and didn't know that I had a Jeweler in my life that was dropping jewels for me to catch. I cared too much about who liked me and how I could keep them near. I was too busy trying to keep those who cared nothing about me but cared more about what I had to offer them close. I call those leeches. They were sucking the blood right out of me, and for a while, that became my norm. I explained to my mentor, I was so busy listening to everyone about my life, marriage, ministry, and more that I became unstable. I was trying to be everything to everybody, while still figuring out what and who I was for myself. To be honest, I lost myself in the midst. I wrote all of this to tell you that everyone's advice for your life is not what you need. Due to everyone telling me what I should do with my life, I felt that I would never receive anything from God regarding ministry, marriage, business, etc. I was praying for what I wanted one minute, but not believing that it could happen to me. I was extremely unstable. I was what the bible calls, double-minded. I know when we all read this we think, “oh this is just for those who don't know if they believe in God or not.” Sorry to break it to you, but it can be you too. Especially if you are praying one minute and worrying the next. You believe there is a God; however, you don't think he can fix your issue or that you are worthy of His love. When we do things like this, we become unstable in all our ways. I felt like I was going wherever the wind blew. God doesn't want that for our lives. He doesn't want us to be confused. God is about clarity. Indecision is of the devil. Stand firm on what God says! When we doubt God, we invite the enemy in with his spirit of indecision and confusion. As a result, we are unsure of ourselves. We bring that instability into our purpose, identity, health, finances, ministry, family, and even work environment. The devil is not thinking about where you are at the moment; he is focused on where he can get you to. One indecisive moment can lead to chaos in your lifestyle. You unknowingly may think, let me ask Mom and Grandma, or Dad and Pastor about what to do with my marriage. Now you have multiple opinions driving you insane on which to follow. You didn't know that entry just caused so much chaos in your family, and now you on your way to divorce court because of one indecisive moment. It's not that they gave you bad advice, but two out of four you ask probably wasn't married, the one that is on their fourth and the last one doesn't even believe in Jesus. To top it none of them have peace about their situation. They were like King Saul trying to give David his armor that didn't even work for him to fight Goliath. (1 Samuel

17:38) In times like this, we must seek God, and he shall direct our path to the righteous and wise counsel we are in dire need. Trust God and Watch He will give you what you need at the proper time.

Just for today, I will surrender to God's direction to wise counsel and not seek out advice from unwise people.

Prayer: Father, I surrender my will to yours. Direct me to those that will speak only what you say. I trust that you will use my confusion for clarity for others and myself. Use me and mature me to be wise counsel for someone else. Thank You!

Day 7

"Do not be deceived, God is not mocked; for whatever a man sows, that he will also reap." Galatians 6:7

Hurt People Hurt People. How many of us have heard this before? I know I have plenty of times. I've had it said to me when I was hurting others unknowingly. I recently had this conversation with my daughter. She was upset about the actions of her friend. She began to take her attitude out on her brother. I explained to her, just as I am explaining to you. What we give out is what we get back. We cannot expect to sow discord and receive love in return. When we plant an apple seed, we get back apples, not oranges. When we sow negativity, we get back negativity, not positivity. For us to receive what we expect, we must first, give it. I know the culture tells us to treat people how they treat us. Nevertheless, scriptures say “to love those as you love yourself.”(Matthew 22:39) Yes, you have to teach people how to treat you by treating them how you want to be treated. Everyone's not taught how to love, be friendly, or show compassion. Most of these qualities are learned from actions witnessed or interpreted from responses given. Even so, if we want love, we must first show love. So let's begin to change the stigma of "Hurt people hurt people." Let's start to represent change, love, heal, wholeness, peace, and more amazing vibes. Changed people change people. Healed people heal people. Delivered people deliver people. Saved people save people. Helped people help people.

Forgiven people forgive people. Loved people love people. Let's change the trajectory of what the world says and be people of the WORD.

Just for today, I will not be afraid to enjoy what is beautiful. I will believe that I shall receive a Bountiful Harvest for the Bountiful Seed I've sown. I will treat people how I want to be treated.

Prayer: Father, Thank you! Thank you for sowing into me love, joy, peace, longsuffering, kindness, goodness, faithfulness, gentleness, and self-control. I know to take what you gave me and sow into your people. Father, help me be a representation of you and your amazing qualities. For your Word says that what I sow, I shall also reap. I thank you in advance. In Jesus' name. Amen!

Day 8

"So David inquired of the Lord, saying, 'Shall I pursue this troop? Shall I overtake them?' And He answered him, 'Pursue, for you shall surely overtake them and without fail recover all.'" 1 Samuel 30:8

Today is the 8th day, and biblically 8 means New Beginnings. Today is your day to pursue all that God has set for you. For one whole year, I sat and waited for what God said was mine. I kept making it about everyone and everything else but myself. I said well so-and-so was holding me up. Then God removed so-and-so from my life. Then my excuse was I need a permanent job. I received that and more. Finally, my mentor asked me, why are you sitting and not pursuing what God called you to be? My response was another excuse; well, I was trying to be obedient and respect the order of things. I thought maybe the gift would come to me. I thought I sounded sincere, but in all reality, I was scared. It wasn't that I wasn't ready; it was my fear of rejection and admittedly fear of success. It was always if I pursue this that so and so would leave me, or that people wouldn't like who I had become. I know to seek what God called me to be, meant growth and maturity. We all know with growth and maturity comes separation and severing of ties with the immature. Here is David, a man whose heart was after God. Yet, David had some insecurity and some sinful natures. Having said that, God told him to pursue what He had for him and watch how he would overtake them. I get it, the business is above your league, but what did God say? The ministry will cost you some friends and family, but what did God say? The marriage will cause you to grow up and growing hurts, but what did God say? I know you were comfortable in that box, but what did God say? It is time for you to get up and go after what God has for you. He has already released it; He is just waiting for you to get up and go after it. My encouraging words for you today are what my mentor said to me, PURSUE IT!

Just for today, I will pursue what God has for me.

Prayer: Jesus, forgive me for living beneath the standards you set for me. Lord, forgive me for not moving when you said go. I know delayed obedience is still disobedience, forgive me for disobeying. Lord, give me the stamina and

strength to go after what you said was mine. Remove every spirit of fear. I know that you have not given me a spirit of fear but of love, power, and a sound mind. I thank you in advance for staying with me and already declaring me victorious. I pray this in Jesus' name. Amen!

Day 9

"But You, O Lord, are a shield for me, My Glory and the One who lifts up my head."

Psalm 3:3

Depression is real. In 2014, the late talented Robin Williams was found in his California home, hanging. This brilliant actor who helped everyone else laugh in his movies, Mrs. Doubtfire, Aladdin (1992 version), and Jumanji to name a few, was a victim of depression, which led to his suicide. It pained my heart to read the news of his death. I was a fan of his and his work. I know there have been other celebrities who suffered from depression, but for some reason, Robin Williams hit home for me. I am not sure if it was because I was a fan or the fact that I, too, was suffering from it. Many times depression became so overwhelming that I couldn't get out of bed. I didn't want any light in my room. I didn't want to eat and at times, I didn't want to live. I am not sure how many of you have suffered, but I know you are not alone. I would like to first say to you, please seek help. Therapy has been a tremendous blessing to me. I know what it feels like to have a big heavy coat weighing you down and it seems like it just won't stop raining. However, our faith is in Jesus, who stated that we are more than overcomers. November 3rd, 2018, I was under so much pressure. I was depressed. I was walking around like a zombie with a deceiving smile on my face. My husband was in jail again, my finances were dwindling, my kids hated me, and I was getting bullied badly at work from an elder lady. To top it, I felt embarrassed and that church folk was judging my situation, again. I was ready to end it and jump in front of a moving train. I was ready to take my life. When the time presented itself, my coworker started to have a conversation with me that made me forget all about the train. When I got home, I cried a great deal. I was willing to let life circumstances coerce me into wanting to kill myself. God is and was a shield. When I read today's scripture, I was reminded of my coworker, who happened to talk to me as soon as it was time for me to jump. Not only did God shield me from making a horrible and selfish move through her; He also allowed me to find joy in life again from that moment. God has more for us and allowing depression to take us from what God has for us is not the way to go out. Just imagine all of the good that you will miss. God is a lifter of the head, especially in times of depression. Make the enemy mad by lifting your head when you feel down and depressed. You do not always have to be strong. It is okay to be weak. For where you are weak, God is strong!

Just for today, I will keep my head lifted high. I will surrender to God's shield.

Prayer: Thank you, Jesus, for being the lifter of my head. Thank you for shielding me from irrational decisions and thinking. Father, give me the strength to endure in this season of trials and tribulations. Father, thank you because it could have been another way. Yet, you are a keeper even when we do not want to be kept! Thank you! I will

forever give your name the praise and glory that it is due. I pray this in Jesus' name, Amen!

Suicide Prevention Hotline: 1-800-273-8255

Day 10

"Enter into His gates with thanksgiving, And into His courts with praise. Be thankful to Him, and bless His name. For the Lord is good; His mercy is everlasting, And His truth endures to all generations." Psalm 100:4-5

This morning, I woke up and began to weep before the Lord. This cry wasn't the usual weeping I had done before. This cry was the weeping of a grateful child. Many moments we get so caught up with what has been going wrong that we forget to use our manners. We forget to say "Thank you" for the things that could be going wrong or should be. I woke up on my daughter's birthday and instead of being upset that my husband was incarcerated, being upset that for eight months I had to be a single parent, or that in a few months 2019 would be over; I woke up with an attitude of Thank You! I was in a different place than I was last year. Sometimes we dwell so much on what is not happening that we become the face of ungratefulness. Look back over your life and think of all the things that happened. Now, think of all the things that could have made that worse. Did it happen? No, it did not! Be grateful! Now, look at all the things that God brought you through and still bringing you to. I didn't have the same story as many other incarcerated wives. I wasn't struggling, my kids were doing well, and I wasn't depressed, as I had been before in this situation. I had refused to let the enemy have his way of making me feel or play the victim. I knew that my attitude of gratitude would give the enemy a black eye. Many don't realize, but the enemy wants you to be depressed and oppressed. He wants to steal your joy. Scripture says, "Resist the devil, and he will run away from you." (James 4:7b) When the enemy is spitting lies about your identity or reminding you of the wrong happening; grab an attitude of gratitude and begin to thank Jesus for everything! My mother always said, "Having manners can take you far." I love to hear my children say "please" and "thank you." It pains me when I hold the door for someone, and they don't say, "Thank You." So it is in this spirit, our father loves to hear you say "Thank you." Remember to use your manners, especially when the enemy comes to you with depression and oppression. But most importantly, when Jesus allows you to see another day.

Just for today, I will have an attitude of gratitude.

Prayer: Jesus, THANK YOU! You have been so good to me! You have been better than I have been to myself! Thank you for everything! You did not have to let me live another day, but you did, and for that, I give you thanks! Amen!

Day 11

"As iron sharpens iron, so friends sharpen each other's faces." Proverbs 27:17

"Fix your crown; it was hanging!" This quote, my good girlfriend said to another close friend of mine in our "Winning Circle" group text. We were thrilled with all the fantastic things that were happening in our lives. At the moment, we were celebratory of each other and how God had brought us through some rough patches in our lives. If I could tell you the stories behind us ladies, you would be praising God right along with us. Many would say it was a dysfunction that brought us together; nevertheless, it was God who ordained the relationship. For many years I was plagued with the thought of me never having friends. I was going through friends just as a baby goes through diapers. I just wasn’t comfortable with friendships. Due to the fact of my lack of trust in people, friends came harder than I expected as I got older. I had friends who betrayed me so many times that I just gave up the idea of obtaining genuine friendships. It wasn't that I didn't have associates; I just didn't have real friendships. I knew plenty of people, but they were not my confidants. But thank God for growth! The close friends I have now been here for almost seven years. This is a long time compared to my track record. If I can be honest, I was not mature enough for friendship. Being that I am the youngest of the group, I still had my temper tantrums over childish things. Per contra, growth happened. Now I can say that I can sharpen them as they sharpen me. Friendships like this require vulnerability and accountability. There is no way to get around that and still be able to be sharpened. You can't be sharpened unless you are vulnerable to say, I struggle with this thing. Those friends you are connected to should be able to tell you when you are doing something wrong. Friendships should not devalue your character, it should enhance your lifestyle. Friendships should help you see things from different points of view. Let's not forget that friendships require work on both ends, just like any relationship. It is an old saying, show me your friends and I will show you your future. God will place the right ones around that will sharpen you as you sharpen them.

Just for today, I will be friendly. I will be supportive and loving to the people who God has

placed in my life. I will strengthen those around me as they strengthen me.

Prayer: Father, help me to be friendlier. Your word says those who want friends should first show themselves friendly. I pray for divine connections within my friendships. Allow me to be used to bring glory to your name in my friendships. Lord, give me the strength to strengthen my friendships as you provide them with the power to strengthen me. Thank you for every association that comes from you.

Day 12

"And let us not grow weary while doing good, for in due season we shall reap if we do not lose heart." Galatians 6:9

On January 23, 2017, I got a phone call that a woman in a black truck ran my husband off the highway where he smashed my vehicle into a pole. Of course, I was thankful that I didn't receive a call saying my husband was dead or hurt, but I must admit I was upset that this woman decided to keep driving. In my head, all I could think was another great financial burden with this car. Have you ever felt like the enemy was trying to run you off the road and leave you with the mess to clean up? Like hit you and then run so your insurance skyrocket?

Despite the fact it just happened to my husband, I felt like I was getting hit by the enemy during the entire month of January 2017. Between multiple runs to the shop because of car trouble, financial issues, marriage problems, business issues, and my kids acting crazy, I could not seem to make it to the address I placed in my GPS , Victory. I went from living in the overflow in November to barely making it in January. I did not understand what was going on. All I knew was I was determined to keep going. I refused to quit when I knew I had 11 months left in the year to get things together. I felt like I was getting attacked on all ends. I didn't know whether I made a wrong move or was this just the backlash from the enemy because I was aligning myself with greater. I knew the steps I was making were of God, so I knew I wasn't disobedient. I was doing everything I heard him say. However, I was getting beat up on something terrible. Then it all hit me like the car hit my husband. I was experiencing things that were teaching me lessons. I wasn't just coasting in life, but I was experiencing life. I was experiencing the wrong things so that I would know what was right for me and my journey. I had decided not to let life work me, but that I work my life. I had to remind myself that I am a spiritual being having natural experiences. So, I permitted myself to go forward. I permitted myself to be free. I allowed myself to love myself fully. Yet, I also knew that I had to experience the setback to get the setup for a great comeback. Things were going wrong, but I was not going to go with them.

So I ask you today, how are you handling you? Are you living as a natural being having spiritual experiences or vice versa? I challenge you to live for your future and not for your current circumstances. Only 10% of your life is what happens, 90% is how you react. So how will you respond? Will you stay in the broken car on the side of the road where the enemy hit you or will you tow the car to get a new tire and fix whatever needs to be adjusted so that you can get to where you need to be? Stay faithful in doing good and watch how your new "car" will be blessed.

Just for today, I will press forward. I will not give up, no matter what the enemy throws my way.

Prayer: Father, thank you! Thank you for your strength to press forward. I will continue because I know that the race is not given to the swift nor the

strong but to the one who endures. I shall survive like a good soldier in Jesus' name. Amen!

Day 13

"Lord, teach me your way. I will walk in your truth. Make my heart united when I think of your name." Psalm 86:11

So recently, I received an invite to a job interview with the agency I work with. I decided not to go and went to work. However, once I got to work, I received a job interview with the federal government. A job that I wanted. It was Washington, D.C., and that meant that I would not receive time for going on this interview. I was sitting here debating on how I could receive time for this federal interview. All these thoughts of lying came into my mind. Maybe if I said the one I was supposed to attend today was rescheduled. As soon as I was about to submit a false time slip, I was convicted and thought of all the bad things that could happen. Instead, I ripped it up and filed just my time for my next doctor's appointments. Deep down, I was so mad that I had to give up a job interview that I wanted all because I believed in karma.

Let's be honest, many of us would not have done the right thing. We would have prayed for God to cover us as we lied, prayed for the job, got the job, and then said God gave it to us. No sir, no ma'am, not at all. Our lying got us that job. As bad as we want things, we must remember to go about it God's way. I am inclined to believe that if we have to struggle with the idea of going to get something, it's not from God. In God's Word are his ways. We choose to walk in the truth or not. God gave us free-will.

When the interview came up, all I can think of was "What would Jesus Do." You know the old WWJD. I struggled with the thought I would lie my way there, and then God would let me lose my job as consequences. Every action has a reaction.

So while this may not be as uplifting as you want it to be but telling the truth goes a long way. Jesus says he is the truth and the light. Why would I risk my integrity for a job that God is possibly saying No about? Think about that when the next event or item is a struggle. Be honest with yourself and the people around you. Integrity opens doors that lying can't.

Just for today, I will be honest with myself and those around me.

Prayer: Thank you, Lord, for the gift of truth. Your word says that the truth will set me free. Father, forgive me for every lie I have ever told and instill in me the truth and your truth. Thank you for setting us free from all lies that could damage the walk we have with you. I pray this in Jesus' name, Amen!

<u>Day 14</u>

"For we are His workmanship, created in Christ Jesus for good works, which God prepared beforehand that we should walk in them." Ephesians 2:10

Our lives may not be going the way we planned it, but it is going exactly the way God intended it. I know many of you are thinking, well what about all the mistakes I've made. Yup, He also wrote those mistakes within. God knew all the mistakes we would make, all the trial and error, and all the beautiful things we do. Your life was all in God's plan. Many times when I messed up on something I figured let me throw it away and start over. That's not God's plan for us. He knew some things we would mess up and thank God he doesn't throw us away and make a new one of us. The thing about it is, He could do that being that he is the Almighty Creator of Life. Yet, He gives us chance after chance to get things right. Thank God for another chance because I blew a few of them writing this devotional.

We must remind ourselves that anything we do that is not going according to our plan cannot stop the will of God. Sorry, but we are not that powerful. My pastor says that God incorporates our mistakes into our miracles. As an imperfect being, that is amazing to hear. It's incredible to know that even my imperfections cannot stop the plans or the blessing that He spoke over my life. I am reminded that even though I messed up relationships, jobs, homes, cars, time and of course, blew so much money on unnecessary items, that it's all working together. Romans 8:28-30 says, "And we know that all things work together for good to those who love God, to those who are the called according to His purpose. For whom He foreknew, He also predestined to be conformed to the image of His Son, that He might be the firstborn among many brethren. Moreover, whom He predestined, these He also called; whom He called, these He also justified; and whom He justified, these He also glorified." God already predestined my mistakes into his plan for my life.

Remember, we are all part of God's plan.

Just for today, I will understand that my mistakes are all part of God's plan. I will not think that

highly of me that I can damage the program God has for my life.

Prayer: Father, forgive me for thinking that I can damage the plan you have for my life with my imperfections. Thank you, Lord, for giving me confidence in you. That even in my flaws that you can still use me for your glory. Thank you, Lord! Have your way in my life today. I trust you fully! I love you! In Jesus' name, I pray, Amen!

Day 15

"Therefore humble yourselves under the mighty hand of God, that He may exalt you in due time, casting all your care upon Him, for He cares for you." 1 Peter 5:6-7

My son and I were taking the bags of groceries into the house one afternoon. I called myself trying to grab everything, so I wouldn't have to come back out. I lifted all the heavy bags and gave my son all the, so what I thought easy bags. One of the bags I considered to be comfortable was too heavy for my son. When I gave him the bag, he said, "Mommy, It's too heavy to carry with all the bags I have." I thought to myself why he didn't just ask me to carry it for him. I said to him, "J, give me the bag. It's not too heavy for me to carry." Him being the sweet loving son that he is, he hesitated, looked at all the bags I was carrying and shocked his head no and struggled to carry it.

How many of us looked at how I first did and said, "Awww, he's so sweet." Of course, I thought he was trying to be the sweet, tough guy. However, I thought of all the times I didn't ask God to take the hard thing. I would rather struggle with my care that was too heavy for me to carry instead of casting it on the Caretaker, Jesus Christ. Some of us may have taken the mindset of my son, J and think Jesus has all these cares in the world that he is handling. This baggage is something I can manage. When, in reality, we cannot handle it alone. Pardon me, but that's not your job!

Scripture tells us to cast our cares simply because Jesus cares. I get so confused when people decided to vent all their issues to someone who does not care for them instead of venting to someone who not only tells them they care but repeatedly shows them they care. It's like we constantly self-sabotage ourselves by carrying around baggage that we do not have to carry. Brother, Sister, Free yourself. Take every weight that you have, and cast them onto the Father. You will not be able to move forward with the weight that you are carrying.

In this same story, because of all the bags, I was carrying; I was not able to open the door to my home. Many of you are trying to get through a door, but you must release the baggage to turn the knob. Release those bags to God and walk in your freedom.

Just for today, I will cast all my cares unto the Lord, for He cares for me.

Prayer: Lord, I am releasing everything that has weighed me down. I release every care onto you. I lift my hands and surrender so that I can walk through the doors you have for me, freely. I release everything in Jesus' name, Amen!

Day 16

"The entrance of Your words gives light; It gives understanding to the simple."

Psalm 119:130

Imagine yourself walking in a dark foggy field. You are trying to get to the place called Purpose, but for some odd reason, you feel lost. It doesn't help that you are in a dark field with fog all around. However, you see a small tiny light in front of you. What would you do? Would you stay where you are? Would you begin to run towards it? Would you cry out for help?

Many of us are at this place in life. We see the light, but all the fog has us feeling lost. The fog of life worries has us feeling like the light we see is so tiny when it could just be the fog dimming the light. In situations like this, God is waiting for us to move forward to him. The closer we get to the light, the more the fog disappears. I have never seen a car stop driving because it was fog. Many cars keep pushing until they get where they are going. The more fog there is, the more God requires you to trust Him.

The fog can be your sickness, your financial debt, and or your relationships. The mist is anything that has you feeling like there is no clarity to your vision. God has requested you to place your hands in his as He guides you to the light. He does not require you to know it all at once. What he is asking you to do is take a step of Faith closer to the light.

For the scripture says in John 8:12, "I am the light of the world. He who follows Me shall not walk in darkness, but have the light of life." I dare you to take a deep breath, give your hand to the Father and let Him guide you into the light. He will not let you down.

Just for today, I will trust God and take a step to His light. I will move forward with him even when I cannot see anything but fog.

Prayer: Jesus, thank you! Thank you that even in my foggy situations, I am still alive to experience it. Lord, I trust you fully. Guide me into the levels you have for me.

Day 17

"Let this mind be in you which was also in Christ Jesus." Philippians 2:5

If it isn't one thing, it's another. You will never have a problem-free life. That means what you are dealing with would still come; something would always happen; trials and tribulations would even enter into your life. It's not exactly what's happening in your life; it's how you are responding to it. What I've learned in my road to my 30th Birthday was to stop majoring in the minors. Many times it's the minor issues that pile up that shook my world. If I handle the problems as they came, I wouldn't have to deal with 99 issues all at once. It's mismanagement of trials that causes us depression, anxiety, frustration, and all those negative feelings we have.

We must switch our minds to not feeling like the circumstance is here to hurt us but to strengthen us. It's like going to a gym and working out something that we never worked out before. In the end, our bodies will hurt. However, this is normal because we will be working on something that was never used before. If we continue this process that pain will soon become a muscle used and improved. However, if we stop going, it can later become extra fat causing us to suffer in life. Training yourself in the gym will hurt but only for a little while. The disciple will not only help physically but also emotionally, mentally, and most importantly, spiritually.

The pain of discipline and results of management is better than suffering from the pain of disappointment and no results at all. Discipline allowed me to manage the trials as they came. When situations been to spiral downhill, I would do what I could and give God the rest. I refused to have a stroke or heart attack over cases that were out of my control. By no means, I am not saying you can't have a breakdown. However, what I am saying is have your breakdown as you breakthrough. Keep pushing; keep moving forward. Cry and Pray. Weep and Worship. It's no reason why you can't come out on top. God has already given you victory. Remember you are fighting from victory and not for victory.

Just for today, I will have the mind of Christ. I will remind myself that some issues are only meant to make me who God called me to be.

Prayer: Father, give me patience. Lord help me understand what you want me to see in every circumstance. Open my mind to more. Open my heart to more. Increase my territory and my mental capacity to handle all you have for me. I thank you in advance! Amen!

Day 18

"I press toward the goal for the prize of the upward call of God in Christ Jesus."

Philippians 3:14

Don't you dare give up! You are almost finished! I know for myself, I get almost to the last few chapters of the book and then place the book down. I have to push myself to finish. This world is full of those who start something and never finish. However, we are FINISHERS! I know how hard it can be to finish things. This year, I have been determined to finish everything I start. Now that I have been able to finish things, my goal now is to finish strong! Many times we end weak and have the attitude of well at least I finished. God doesn't want us to finish; He wants us to Finish Strong!

Pressing forward to the prize takes us being persistently consistent and consistently persistent. We have many reasons why we can't do things. However, being persistent means, I am determined that I will make it. Consistency means to keep going until I get to where my goal is. I believe we all have the spirit of consistency in us. I know for myself, I was consistent with being lazy, impatient, and unfinished. Nevertheless, I had to be persistent with being consistent in finishing and committed to growing in Christ.

We all grow; how we produce is the question. Never doubt the fact of you growing. Things that do not change usually die. Stagnation brings about death. So if you are still breathing, still moving, then you are still growing. What I want you to do is move forward! Press forward!

Granted, moving forward means that some parts of you will die. However, your vision must be better than your resume. We must be cautious about not wanting to change, especially as believers. We all have a price to pay to get where we want to be. Even if that means letting go of things, places, and or people. I would rather sacrifice who I am to yield it to who I am going to be. Rather than sacrifice who I shall become because I do not have the value of the process I am. Yes, change is uncomfortable yet; it is not painful. However, to become who God called us to mean pressing out of our comfort zone.

I understand that getting out of the comfort zone can be scary. Being in the place of the unknown can cause fear of failure and success. This is the place where our defensive mechanism of fight or flight pops up. However, the unknown place is a place of Trust. Trusting God and pressing forward produces a manifestation of promises.

Just for today, I will press toward the goal for the prize of the upward call of God in Christ Jesus.

Prayer: Lord, Thank you for the push. Help me to endure in the process. Help me to press towards the prize, which is the call in Christ Jesus. I surrender my ways to your ways. Have your way, In Jesus' name. Amen!

Day 19

"Death and life are in the power of the tongue, And those who love it will eat its fruit." Proverbs 18:21

"Watch your mouth!" As a young adult, I picked up an ugly trait of cursing. It had gotten so bad that those three words we were told to me every day. I tried to break the habit with a curse jar in the house. Of course, it didn't work because I had more curse words than I had money at the time. My husband said to me one day, "Is there anything else in your vocabulary other than curse words." At the moment, I felt tiny. However, it made me look at myself because I was not the person who looked like she cursed like a sailor. That wasn't my character. It especially was not who I wanted to be in life. I had to make a conscious decision to stop. Then one day, I read this scripture. It had me thinking what if my curse words were the cause of my problems in life. For the scripture does say every word I spoke was technically the fruit I was eating. I was eating what I spoke and wondered why it was bitter.

If I wanted to live better, that meant I would have to start talking better. And we all know if you wish better, you have to do better. Now that I knew better, it was time that I did better. Now I will not lie to you and say that I never curse. However, what I will say is that I choose to speak life more than death. Jesus is still working on me too. If we want a better experience than we have to start talking as if we already have it.

In many airports, I see this slogan, "If you see something, say something." Many times we live in a life like this. We wait until we see something positive happening for us to begin to speak positively. However, I believe that if we turned it around, then we would see more. So from now on live life as, "If I say something, I will see something." Speak life and watch life manifest. Speak life over your finances, health, relationships, and watch God turn it around.

Just for today, I will speak life over everything! I will watch my mouth!

Prayer: Jesus, thank you for life. Thank you for giving me the power in my tongue that speaks life and death. I declare life over my finances, my relationships, my health, my family, and

everything I put my hands on. I speak death to everything that is not like you that is connected to me. I decree that my life will be the fruit of every positive word I speak in Jesus' name. Amen!

Day 20

"But let patience have its perfect work, that you may be perfect and complete, lacking nothing." James 1:4

This scripture was my Pastor's favorite when it came to me. He sent this scripture to me so often. I never understood why. All I knew was James 1:4 was surely to be in a response from him to me, especially when I became impatient with my process. As a millennial, patience is not my cup of tea. Many of us want our promises in a microwave form. However, life doesn't permit it that way. When I knew I was called to preach the Word, I thought I would do Ministers in Training classes for one, maybe two years and then become a minister.

Well, it didn't quite work that way. I was in minister classes for possibly three years, but I was in training for almost 5 to 6 years. The training part sucked, but it was worth it all.

Now that I look back, I am glad I never became a minister at that time. I would have embarrassed myself, my family, my Pastor, my church, and God would NOT have been glorified. At the time, I just thought my Pastor didn't like me. (This was my rejection issues.) Now, I know that he loves me dearly. He knew that if I came out of my process before time, I would have been clearly uncooked and possibly given others salmonella. I was not complete and lacking much. I am not saying you must be perfect to be a leader. What I am saying is that you should not have specific spirits, such as lack, in your life to try and pour into someone else.

What exactly are you pouring if you are lacking? If you are full of holes, you have nothing to pour because you cannot contain anything.

God's will for our lives is not to lack. Psalm 23:1 states, "The Lord is my shepherd; I shall not want." To decree bold statements as this means you know precisely who you are and whose you are. Meaning, you know you have no spirit of lack upon your life because everything you need and want is in Christ Jesus. However, a sense of lack causes you to live in a mind of poverty. The title would be more for self-gratification than God's glory. To be at this place takes patience as it says in James 1:3, "knowing that the testing of your faith produces patience." Testing is necessary. The experiment produces perseverance. The patience manifests completion. I declare that you are entering a season of No Lack and that your testing will not be in vain.

Just for today, I will have patience. I will submit to the process, knowing that I will soon be complete and have no lack!

Prayer: Lord, I thank you for the trial. For in the testing I can decree that I am entering into a season of No lack. I shall live in abundance. Thank you for the testing of my faith. I decree I will be mature, complete, and lacking nothing in Jesus' name. Amen!

Day 21

"Now the Lord blesses the latter days of Job more than his beginning;" Job 42:12a

I remember receiving a letter for a new position, and it said, "The Office of Personnel Services and benefits has certified your name for the position described below."

God has certified your name for the promise.

I received an email from the Human Resources Department of my current job before I started stating, "This is to notify you that your name has been certified by The Office of Personnel for the position of…" I was so excited to receive this email because I had been applying for jobs so long that I started to forget what I applied for since nothing was coming. This email was telling me that a higher person certified that my name was the name chosen. Imagine receiving a letter from heaven saying something similar. "This is to notify you that The Office of Personnel has certified your name for the blessing of…" I am sure you would be jumping for joy. Especially if you experienced a Job's trial. You lost everything. Family is gone, money gone and to top it off you are sick. And then you get this email. I have come to declare to you today at the very end of this 21-day that your latter shall be greater. You have wept, travailed, fasted, prayed, and even done the work in this book. God has noticed your sacrifice, and He is here to tell you that He has a blessing with your name on it.

If no one tells you, I want to tell you that I am proud of the person you have become. You have done your best. You have pushed through, and now it is time to give birth to the better you. You are victorious and never forget that. You have fought these past years for victory. You are already winning. It is time you fight from victory. You already have it! You have prayed to get where you are right now. Would you have expected you to be where you are right now? I am proud of you. This is your winning season. It is your turn and your time!

Just for today, I will walk in the victory that is already mine.

Prayer: Jesus, THANK YOU!

Made in the USA
Middletown, DE
28 January 2024

48083743R00057